One Rib Publications

Nassau, The Bahamas

www.oneribpublications.com

oneribpublications@gmail.com

Understanding the Baptism of the Holy Spirit and Speaking in Tongues

Copyright © 2023 by David Burrows

Published 2023 by One Rib Publications

ISBN: 9781959806127

TABLE OF CONTENTS

UNDERSTANDING
BAPTISM
IN THE
HOLY
SPIRIT
AND
SPEAKING
IN
TONGUES

DAVID BURROWS

UNDERSTANDING BAPTISM IN THE HOLY SPIRIT AND SPEAKING IN TONGUES

INTRODUCTION

One of the most misunderstood topics in the church is what is Baptism in the Holy Spirit and what is Speaking in Tongues. In this book my desire is to make clear what is the purpose, application and process for receiving Baptism in the Holy Spirit, Speaking in Tongues, the daily application on the personal level and the proper use of this and the associated gifts of the Holy Spirit in the Church.

In today's world, Holy Spirit Baptism and Speaking in Tongues are often referred to as "The Pentecostal Experience". The Holy Spirit and Pentecost are two different things that converged to mark the date of the entry of the Holy Spirit into the personal lives of believers (the Holy Spirit was present previously but not resident).

Pentecost Sunday is 50 days after the resurrection. It is a pivotal day in the history of the world. It is one of the most important days ever in recorded history, because it was the day when the Kingdom mission was established. When the disciples got together Jesus told them to wait to get together, this is going to be the official launch of the Kingdom. This is where you really begin moving. It is a very important day.

Chapter 1

THE PROMISE

Jesus said if you love me keep my Commandments. He was talking to His disciples. As He was preparing to depart the Earth He said if you love me keep my Commandments. He said I will pray to the Father and He will give you another helper. If He is going to give you another helper then who is the helper?

What Jesus is talking about here is a mystery to the disciples. It was a mystery to the people in that day. I am sure they were confused. In John 14:16-17 Jesus explained,

> *"I will ask the Father, and He will give you another Helper, that He may be with you forever; that is*

the Spirit of truth, whom the world cannot receive, because it does not see Him or know Him, but you know Him because He abides with you and will be in you"

The disciples were thinking, what do you mean you are going to send another Helper, he is with you and then he is going to be in you? You know it didn't make sense to them because they didn't know what was the personal role of the Holy Spirit. He said, I will not leave you orphans. I will come to you. A very powerful statement. He is saying that if I leave you and I do not send the Holy Spirit you will be orphans on the earth. You will not have a parent. You will not have anyone to teach you. To guide you. To direct you through life. Jesus was explaining that the Holy Spirit is important and critical to the mission of the Gospel of the Kingdom of God that Jesus often spoke about.

John 15:26 reads,

"But when the Helper comes whom I will send to you from the Father the Spirit of Truth who proceeds from the Father He will bear witness about me".

What Jesus is saying here is that the Holy Spirit is coming and the Holy Spirit is coming to bear witness of me. He said I have been with you all at this time. You have seen miracles. You have seen all these things. I have given you teaching. I have given you information. I am going to leave but when I leave, I am leaving myself in the form of a Helper with you who will help you. You will not be helpless. You will not be in the world and be helpless because,

"When the Helper comes whom I will send to you from the Father the Spirit of Truth who proceeds from the Father He will bear witness about me".

The Holy Spirit is confirmation of Jesus' existence and validation of everything he shared with the disciples. The Holy Spirit confirms everything that Jesus said. The Holy Spirit is important because Jesus is one with the Spirit.

Sometimes we think Pentecost is a spirit. Pentecost means 50 days. It comes from the Greek word pentekoste which means fiftieth. It was a special celebration of harvest, which happened 50 days after Passover. So Pentecost itself is not important. What is important is what happened at Pentecost after Jesus left. **Fifty 50 days after Jesus left, the official arrival of the Helper came into the earth.**

At Pentecost, when the disciples were all in one accord Jesus had promised this Helper would be with them and everyone who had come into the Kingdom at Pentecost. It was the official what you would call a commissioning. It was the official entry point for the work of the Holy Spirit on a direct personal level. It was the beginning of a new era.

The beginning of the Holy Spirit era. This was the first time that the Holy Spirit would actually live in people. Up until this time, the Holy Spirit was contained in Jesus. Therefore, wherever Jesus went the Holy Spirit went. The Holy Spirit did not do works in other parts; He only did works wherever Jesus was. Now at Pentecost the official ministry of the Holy Spirit was launched and that launching was a game changer.

Chapter 2

THE ARRIVAL

Now we go to the Book of Acts and we see this situation unfolding. In Acts 1:4-5 it says,

> *"Gathering them together, He commanded them not to leave Jerusalem, but to wait for what the Father had promised, "Which," He said, "you heard of from me; for John baptized with water, but you will be baptized with the Holy Spirit not many days from now."*

Jesus rose from the dead. He brought the disciples together and He said do not depart from Jerusalem but wait. He said the Holy Spirit is coming, just wait on Him wait until the appointed time. Wait for the promise of the father, which He said you have heard from Me. He said I have been talking about this. I have been preparing you. There is another Helper coming. I have been preparing you for the release of the Holy Spirit into the earth. He said now go wait.

He said you have heard from me in Acts 1:5

"For John baptized with water, but you will be baptized with the Holy Spirit not many days from now."

He said you know John did a Baptism and John's Baptism was good but this Baptism is different. This is the Holy Spirit Baptism. Holy Spirit Baptism is important to a believer because believers are baptized into Jesus in the water. But there is a second Baptism, when you are baptized into the Holy Spirit. It releases and activates a new element in us. This Baptism is characterized by the word "dunamis", like dynamite, indicating a release of power.

Acts 1:8

> *"But you will receive power when the Holy Spirit has come upon you, and you will be my witnesses in Jerusalem and in all Judea and Samaria, and to the end of the earth."*

Jesus was preparing them because they had a mistaken conception of his mission. They thought he came to overthrow the Roman Government. The scripture speaks of a conversation in Acts 1:6

> *Therefore, when they had come together, they asked Him, saying, "Lord, will you at this time restore the kingdom to Israel?"*

It says, therefore when they had come together they asked Him saying Lord, will you at this time restore the kingdom to Israel. Now I want you to understand something about the disciples. The disciples were in some ways clueless. They were not intentionally clueless but what Jesus was explaining was so magnanimous it was so magnificent it was beyond human understanding. They were always trying to figure out what is He saying now? What is going to happen now? For them they are thinking that Jesus is going to restore the Kingdom physically. They are not thinking about a spiritual Kingdom. They are thinking about taking over Israel. Then Jesus said to them it is not for you to know the times or the seasons, which the Father has put in His own authority.

Chapter 3

THE RELEASE

Jesus was the helper. He was the one who helped everybody. He was the king of the gravy train. Jesus provided whatever was needed. If you needed help with rent, He provided the rent. If you needed healing, He helped you with healing. If you needed deliverance from demons, He was there to help. He was the helper. He said but I am leaving, so I am going to give you another helper. Jesus said that He might abide with you forever. The spirit of Truth. Then He began to explain to the disciples. He said, whom the world could not receive, because it neither sees Him nor knows Him, but you know Him, for He dwells with you, and will be in you.

Now I am sure that was a difficult concept for the disciples to grasp. They were with Jesus all the time and they were comfortable with Him. Then He says you know I am leaving but I am going to send you somebody to replace Me. I'm sure they were scratching their heads because the concept of the Holy Spirit was not a common concept during that time, in terms of the Holy Spirit dwelling in people.

This experience would be the beginning of a dramatic transformation. He said your lives are going to be changed when the Holy Spirit comes, but in our world today, we don't necessarily have the best understanding of the Holy Spirit.

He says, but you shall receive power when the Holy Spirit has come upon you. Now this is another important aspect of it. **He said the Holy Spirit is a Helper but the Holy Spirit is also power.** Jesus further explained that up until this time, the power was in Me only but now the power is going to be released in you through the Holy Spirit and it is going to cause power to be exhibited in your life.

He says, but you shall receive power when the Holy Spirit has come upon you and you shall be witnesses to me in Jerusalem and in Judea and Samaria unto all the ends of the Earth. So Jesus was telling his disciples when this power comes on you this power will cause you to be witnesses like you have never been witnesses before. We know that once the power of the Holy Spirit came on the disciples they became new people.

Before the Holy Spirit's power came on them, they were afraid fishermen. They had been with Jesus. They had seen a lot of things they were excited but they weren't powerful yet but when the Holy Spirit came and the tongues of fire descended they became powerful individuals to the point where the people said these are they who turn the world upside down.

Acts 2:1-4

> "*When the day of Pentecost had come, they were all together in one place. And suddenly, there came*

from heaven a noise like a violent rushing wind, and it filled the whole house where they were sitting. And there appeared to them tongues as of fire distributing themselves, and they rested on each one of them, and they were all filled with the Holy Spirit and began to speak with other tongues, as the Spirit was giving them utterance."

The Baptism of the Holy Spirit and the power of the Holy Spirit was officially released into the Earth through the disciples. A new era began.

Chapter 4

THE PURPOSE
OF THE HOLY SPIRIT
BAPTISM

When I was growing up, the Holy Spirit was almost like a weird spirit or ghost. It was a nebulous cloud that came into a room causing people to run around and buck their head, or jump over the chairs. The perception was that the Holy Spirit was almost an it; if this gets you then you do weird things. For many people that was their concept of the Holy Spirit. But, to understand the Baptism of the Holy Spirit we must first understand the Holy Spirit.

What or who is the Holy Spirit? Well the Holy Spirit is not an it. The Holy Spirit is a He. The Holy Spirit is actually the Spirit of God. It is not complicated, even though we have complicated it. We only have to understand how the Spirit works in the world and how God works. I want to share with you some things to help to get an understanding. It is somewhat complicated but this example explains and communicates it in layman's terms, this relationship between the Holy Spirit and God.

I saw this statement that somewhat encapsulates who the Holy Spirit is. **He is the creator Spirit, present before the creation of the universe; and through His power, everything was made in Jesus Christ by God the Father.** Now that sounds crazy but if you read the Bible you will consistently see that the Bible talks about the Holy Spirit and Jesus always being present with God and as God. So basically, the Holy Spirit is one of the three expressions of God. God is one, but He is revealed in three different forms.

One example to gain an understanding of this is where you have liquid or you have water and as water goes into the air as it evaporates it becomes gaseous water or water vapor. Then if you freeze it, it becomes solid in the form of ice, but it is still water.

Another example is this. The ocean is the source of the water. That is where all the water is. That is where the mass of water is. God is like the ocean, but the ice is when the water came from the ocean and you were able to touch it. Jesus was like the Iceman. He was the one that you could touch and feel. He was the source, but he came in a form we could identify with and who we could touch. He is God but it is God in a form that you can actually touch and see because you cannot see God. The Bible says no one has seen God but this is a way of revealing what God is like.

The ocean is like God the Father. Father means source. From the ocean, water rises into the air and forms clouds. Clouds are water droplets suspended in the air. It comes from the source and then it comes back down as rain. This is a simplified example of understanding the Holy Spirit. Father means source and sustainer. God is the sustainer of everything. God does not move but the Holy Spirit moves and Jesus moved. In Genesis 1 it says,

"In the beginning God created the heaven and the earth. And the earth was without form, and void; and darkness was upon the face of the deep. And the Spirit of God moved upon the face of the waters."

So, in the beginning, God created the Heaven and the Earth and the Earth was without form and void and darkness was upon the face of the deep and **the Spirit of God moved**. This expression of God moves in different situations.

God is omnipresent. He is everywhere, but His movement is exhibited through the Holy Spirit. It says, and the Spirit of God moved upon the face of the waters. So the Spirit and the Word moved. Jesus moved from heaven and came to Earth. In a way, God moved but God was still in heaven because He is the source. This expression of God says **the Word became flesh and dwelt among us**. God revealed Himself by coming to Earth in flesh so the Word moves and the Spirit moves. The Holy Spirit has always been with us but not in us.

If you read throughout the Old Testament it would say the Spirit of God did this or the Spirit of God did that. The Spirit of God moved on this prophet or this King. **It was a specific movement or activity of the Holy Spirit for an occasion.** The Holy Spirit did not live in these people; he moved on them. So, the Holy Spirit would perform different things or inspire people and people would do things. They would prophesy (like Isaiah or Jeremiah). They would have feats of strength (like Sampson). All of these were by the power of the Holy Spirit but the Holy Spirit was not resident in people.

In fact, the concept of the Holy Spirit being resident didn't come about until Jesus came along. You can characterize it like this. There is uni-presence and then there is omnipresent. Uni-presence means present in a single place. Omnipresent means present everywhere. So the Holy Spirit was characterized by uni-presence in the Old Testament. Then when Jesus came the Holy Spirit became accessible to everyone but was present in Jesus only.

John 15:26 says,

> *"But when the helper comes who I will send to you from the Father the Spirit of Truth who proceeds from the Father He will bear witness about me."*

So He is saying to the disciples when the Spirit comes you are going to recognize Him because everything that I told you and whatever I did He is going to confirm it. He is going to remind you of it. The day of Pentecost was the day when this began. Jesus told the disciples to get together 50 days from the resurrection and go in the Upper Room and something big is going to happen. Something that is going to transform your life. It is going to transform the world. The world will never be the same after this event.

After this event, the Kingdom is officially launched and through the power of attorney, the Holy Spirit is authorized to act on the Earth. In Matthew 3:11 John said,

> *"I baptize you in water, but He will baptize you with the Holy Spirit and fire."*

John began to foretell of some dramatic event that was going to happen. He said I baptized in water. That's great but the one who was coming after me is going to baptize with the Holy Spirit and fire.

Jesus said, John truly baptized with water, but you shall be baptized with the Holy Spirit not many days from now. Jesus was telling the disciples it was coming. The Holy Spirit Baptism is coming. The Holy Spirit is here, but you are going to receive something special. The Gift of the Holy Spirit is a special gift because it transforms your life. You will never be the same, and if you take advantage of it, your life becomes infinitely better.

This is Baptism of the Holy Spirit. Jesus also said, but you shall receive power when the Holy Spirit has come upon you and you shall be witnesses unto me. The gift of the Holy Spirit coincided with the infusion of power. The Holy Spirit is also referred to as "dunamis" or Dynamite power. The Holy Spirit is about power on the Earth. Power to change your life. Power to solve problems. Everything that is needed on the Earth, the Holy Spirit is here to solve it. Whatever is your issue, the Bible says He is a helper and He will give you power or empower you.

Chapter 5

THE RESULT OF THE RELEASE

When you need help, you call the Holy Spirit. Have you ever heard people say the Holy Spirit helped me? Do you need help today to pay your rent? You can say help me Holy Spirit. If you have a problem that you cannot solve you say help me Holy Spirit. That is why the Holy Spirit is here. The Holy Spirit brings the power to impact your life. Then at the day of Pentecost it says then there appeared to them *"divided tongues as a fire and one set on each of them."* This was evidence of what Jesus told them. He told them to gather together. Then when the day was fully come then there was evidence of that activity. It says they were all filled with the Holy Spirit and began to speak with other tongues as the Spirit gave them utterance. This was a sign that the Gift of the Holy Spirit had arrived. They spoke a new language that they did not learn from man.

After Peter said to them repent and be baptized in the name of Jesus and you shall receive the gift of the Holy Spirit, people began to receive this gift and their lives were changed dramatically. Thank God for the Gift of the Holy Spirit. A gift is something that you don't have to work for. You don't have to do anything special. Jesus explained it this way in Luke 11:13

> *"If you then, being evil, know how to give good gifts to your children, how much more will your heavenly Father give the Holy Spirit to those who ask Him?"*

I remember when I was growing up in church people used to go to the altar and really work hard for the Holy Spirit; they used to call it tarrying. They would sit there and they would cry, scream and do all kinds of things. You don't have to go through all that. You just ask and in faith receive and He will give you the Gift of the Holy Spirit. I remember my experience in receiving the Holy Spirit. I didn't really know anything about the baptism in the Holy Spirit and I had just been saved. I had not been to a church in many years.

I was in Tulsa, Oklahoma, as a student at Oral Roberts University. We were at a Kenneth Hagin meeting, somebody laid hands on me and I just fell. This was all new to me. I didn't know what was going on and then I started Speaking in Tongues and I was amazed. Where did this come from? Basically, what happens is that when you pray and you receive this gift, the Speaking in Tongues is a sign of activation. So the Holy Spirit is activated, and the language of Speaking in Tongues is a tool for you to be effective on the Earth for His power to be released in your life. It is a spirit language. Some scholars have speculated that it was the original language in the Garden.

Receiving the Baptism of the Holy Spirit happens by faith, you simply ask in prayer, and God will give it to you; and in faith, you open your mouth and begin to speak with other tongues. For some people it is instantaneous, for others it happens over a period. Never stress about it, just know that if you have asked God he will give to you and you will see the evidence. Do not put a timetable on it. Just walk in faith knowing that God has heard your prayer and you have received it. For some people they prayed and a few days later, they were in a worship service singing and the singing became tongues.

Now I want to share with you how the Holy Spirit transforms your life. Let's begin with the fact that the Holy Spirit transforms your life through power. It is a power gift. It is a gift to empower you. Empower means to make you capable of doing things that you were not able to do before. When someone empowers you, they give you authority. They give you tools. They give you information that helps you to become stronger.

Chapter 6

THE FUNCTION OF THE HOLY SPIRIT

The Holy Spirit Baptism is a power gift. It produces empowerment and once we understand the power of the Holy Spirit, it affects our lives and transforms our lives. In Romans 8:26 there is an indication of how the Holy Spirit Works in us. How it transforms our life. It says,

"Likewise the Spirit also helps us in our weaknesses: for we don't know what to pray for as we ought: but the Spirit Himself makes intercession for us with groanings which cannot be uttered".

So sometimes you start to pray and you don't even know what you are praying. But you begin to pray in the Spirit, praying things that your mind cannot understand or comprehend, but Jesus said I am going to give you another helper. He said this helper is going to help you accomplish whatever you need on the Earth. **The HOLY SPIRIT BAPTISM is a power tool.** How does he power you? Let me give you an example. If you have an electric car, it needs to be charged before it hits the road. Charge is the same word as "edify" which means to build up. Praying in Tongues is about edification, getting you charged up for life ahead.

So if you edified something like an electric car, if you plug it into the socket it charges right? So when you charge something, the same word for that is edified. Back in the day when we used to smoke weed the guys would say I'm going to get a charge. So you get edified. You get charged up. You get high in a spiritual sense. The Holy Spirit is there to get you high, but this is a good high. You can smoke marijuana cocaine, hashish or any kind of drug and none of them can get you as high as the Holy Spirit can get you. I used to do many of those drugs back in the day, many years ago, but guess what, **I found that there is no high like the Most High.**

I made some charges in my life, and then I got charged up by the Holy Spirit; and that's the best high I ever had in my life. This high is so good you don't want to come down. The Holy Spirit edifies us. He charges us up. When you wake up in the morning you say let me go in my closet, let me pray in the Holy Spirit and then all of a sudden you get charged up. That is a part of how the Holy Spirit transforms your life.

The Holy Spirit is there for edification and intercession. Interceding means coming in between, or on behalf of someone. The Holy Spirit is there to edify you, and to provide intercession. What is important to remember about the Holy Spirit is that **there is a private aspect of the Holy Spirit and a public aspect of the Bap-**

tism of the Holy Spirit and Speaking in Tongues and these are very different.

The public aspect is when you operate with the Gift of the Holy Spirit. The Gift of the Holy Spirit includes Speaking in Tongues and interpretation. On the private side, it means you personally Speak in Tongues for your personal edification, intercession, or for whatever you need. You get charged up, and you allow the Holy Spirit through your praying in tongues to intervene and to sort things out on your behalf.

The Apostle Paul, in the book of Corinthians says pursue love and desire spiritual gifts. There are gifts of the Holy Spirit and then there is the **private gift of Speaking in Tongues.** The gifts of the Holy Spirit are for public benefit. There is a private benefit of Speaking in Tongues that is for you personally. When you pray in tongues, you edify yourself, and you intercede. The Bible says pursue love and desire spiritual gifts but especially that you may prophesy. He is talking about when you are in public. If we come in here in public and I just start Speaking in Tongues and I don't give any explanation or anything like that everybody is looking at me like what in the world is he doing. For you to benefit there needs to be an interpretation. But, if you are Speaking in Tongues privately there is no interpretation necessary.

This is what the Apostle Paul explained in 1st Corinthians 14:2

> "*He who speaks in a tongue does not speak to men but to God, for no one understands him; however, in the spirit he speaks mysteries. But, he who prophesies speaks edification and exhortation and comfort to men. He who speaks in a tongue edifies himself, but he who prophesies edifies the church. I wish you all spoke with tongues, but even more that you prophesied; for he who prophesies is greater than he who speaks with tongues, unless indeed he interprets, that the church may receive edification.*

It says for he who Speaks in Tongues does not speak to men but to God. It is telling us that we are speaking to God. This language is a direct connection with God for us to exchange with him in the Spirit. It says for no one understands Him, however, in the Spirit He speaks mysteries. We don't know exactly what we are speaking but we know we are speaking through the Gift of the Holy Spirit. Therefore, you have the personal gifts and then you have the spiritual gifts that are for everybody. It says he who speaks in an unknown tongue **edifies himself.** He who prophesies edifies the church. He goes on to say, I would that you all spoke with tongues but rather that you prophesy in church.

The Apostle Paul is talking about the differences in use. It says greater is He that prophesies than He that Speaks in Tongues except he interprets that the church may receive edifying. So the church is edified in public when we Speak in Tongues and produce an interpretation. It says, for when I pray in tongues my spirit prays. This is a spirit prayer.

This is not a natural human prayer. It says for if I pray, my spirit prays but my understanding is unfruitful. I don't understand what I'm saying, but my spirit is praying and God understands and that's the most important thing.

Here is the thing to remember. Very important. **The Holy Spirit in you is subject to your control.** Some people say the Spirit made me do it as if they didn't have a choice. You always have a choice. **God is not a God of disorder**. Some people say well you know I got up in the middle of the service while the preacher was preaching and I couldn't control myself. The Holy Spirit just came upon me. No the Holy Spirit doesn't operate like that. The Holy Spirit is a gentleman. He will give you power but He will also give you discretion on how to release the power.

Human tradition and ignorance have caused people to give the Holy Spirit a bad name, but we are here today to set the record straight. The Holy Spirit in you is subject to your control. It goes on to say, what is the conclusion then? I would pray with the Spirit sometimes, and I will pray with my understanding sometimes. I will sing in the Spirit sometimes, and I will sing with understanding sometimes. The Apostle Paul was explaining, you know sometimes I pray in the Spirit and sometimes I pray in my understanding. Both tools are available. You use whichever tool is right for the particular occasion.

1 Corinthians 14:14-15 says,

> *"For if I pray in a tongue, my spirit prays, but my understanding is unfruitful. What is* the conclusion *then? I will pray with the spirit, and I will also pray with the understanding. I will sing with the spirit, and I will also sing with the understanding."*

When you can't figure out what to do, just pray in the Spirit because the Spirit is smarter than we are. It says, I will sing with the Spirit, I will also sing with understanding. I thank my God that I Speak with Tongues, more than any of you does. However, in church I would rather speak five words with my understanding that I may teach others than 10,000 words in tongues. He is just explaining that there is a private and a personal use.

Chapter 7

EXAMPLES OF THE HOLY SPIRIT IN ACTION

The gift of the Holy Spirit is for counsel and comfort. When you need something, He is the counselor. He is also referred to by Jesus as the comforter. When you need comfort. When you need counsel. When you need advice. When you need information, the Holy Spirit is there. It says the helper, the Holy Spirit whom the father shall send in my name He will teach you all things and He will **bring to your remembrance** all things that I have said to you.

The Holy Spirit is powerful. I just want to give you a couple illustrations of how the Holy Spirit works. I remember this was years ago my wife and I were having our first child or should I say, she was having our first child. I participated. People are saying, "We got pregnant." I have never been pregnant in my life, and I will never be pregnant so don't confuse me. She was having our first child and I was at the hospital. The nurses said, oh don't worry about it she won't have that baby until tomorrow afternoon. Mind you, she's telling me she's experiencing major pain. That's what she was saying all night. Pain, pain, pain, so I called the nurse in, and the nurse checked her and said to me "she ain't dilated yet, that ain't no real pain yet so don't worry about it. The real pain is coming later. My wife kept saying pain, pain, pain.

After a while, I said, I am going to call the doctor because I don't understand this. I don't know anything about pregnancy, but this does not seem right. I picked up the phone and I went to call our doctor, Dr. Achara. When I called Dr. Achara, his wife said to me he had already left to go to the hospital. She said he got up at four or five o'clock in the morning. He didn't even bathe, he said I have to get to the hospital. I didn't speak to him. I didn't say that there was a problem. So how do you think he knew that there was a problem? It was the Holy Spirit giving him information. He was a very strong believer and what he was doing did not make medical sense.

He came to the hospital and when he came to the hospital, it was about the time the baby was ready to come and within I think maybe 30-40 minutes from the time he came the baby came. My thoughts at the time were to thank God for the Holy Spirit. The nurse was sending me home and I would have gone and left my wife in distress not knowing that something unusual was happening.

I'll tell you another thing that is interesting about the Holy Spirit. This happened a few years ago. Do you remember the hurricane of 2016, Hurricane Matthew? I remember that hurricane vividly. In the aftermath of the hurricane, the Holy Spirit brought some things to my remembrance. I love the Holy Spirit because when you need help He is a helper. I remember I was traumatized. I've been through many hurricanes, but for me, Matthew was the hurricane of hurricanes. I'm comfortable in my house. The generator is on and we are singing and cruising through the storm, everything is good. Suddenly pieces of the roof started flying off. Then the water started coming through. The ceilings collapsed and the house was flooded. The house was devastated.

I have insurance but there is a significant deductible. I'm starting to think, boy what's the deductible on this insurance. How much I will have to come up with personally? I was preparing to buy a car and I'm calculating all these things. How this was going to affect me purchasing a car. I said to my wife let's pray. We prayed in our understanding and we prayed in the Holy Spirit. After we prayed in the Holy Spirit, guess what happened? I went downstairs to a place that I had not been in years. I went through some folders there. I can't even remember why I was going through the folders. I went through the folders and I realized that I had enough money in one of those folders. The money wasn't there but the documents were there telling me that I had enough money to buy the car. The Holy Spirit brought this thing to my remembrance.

I'm sure many of you here today can talk about instances where the Holy Spirit provided you with information that didn't make sense to your natural senses. The Holy Spirit actually gives you business ideas. I remember talking to our Pastors Larry and Joyce, and her talking about this idea for years ahead of time. Suddenly, the idea came to fruition for their business, Louis and Steen's. That had to be a Holy Spirit idea because it didn't make practical sense, and that's what the Holy Spirit does. The Holy Spirit reveals things to you. He gives you information that's not readily accessible. He'll bring things to your remembrance. That's why you have to study the Bible. You have to know the Word and when the Word is in you, the Holy Spirit will activate it.

You may have a situation. You have a big problem and you need some help. You studied the Word and you started to pray in the Holy Spirit in tongues and then all of a sudden you get an answer. You get a solution. He is the Spirit of Truth. If you need truth the Holy Spirit is the Spirit of Truth.

Another important aspect of the Holy Spirit is wisdom and revelation. Sometimes you need wisdom. There are situations and things that happen in your life. Knowledge is good but the Bible says you can get knowledge from a book but to get wisdom you have to get wisdom from God and on the Earth the wisdom of God comes through the Holy Spirit. The Holy Spirit will help you figure out things that you could never figure out on your own. He gives you wisdom.

I remember another incident that happened when I was in hospital for a minor procedure. It was supposed to be routine, just in and out. I was scheduled to stay overnight just as a precaution. Pastor Angie was there with me after the procedure and we are sitting down laughing, and talking, and everything. Then the nurse comes and she says you know we're going to put him to sleep and then you could just come back tomorrow.

She was getting ready to leave. Then **something (the Holy Spirit)** told her she needed to stay. The Holy Spirit said hold on sister don't leave this brother here by himself. So she said to me I am not going home. She called the front desk and turned the semi-private room into a fully private room where she would sleep in the second bed. The lady said no you don't have to be here you should go home. They started arguing. She said I'm paying for this so I'll make the decision. After some debate, the lady said okay you can stay. We got all the paperwork done. She stayed.

I wasn't feeling ill. I was just relaxing. The nurse came in with medication to help me sleep. It was a sleeping pill called Ambien. I did not have a problem sleeping. But hey gave me this sleeping pill. I didn't know what the side effects of the sleeping pill were, but later learned that one of the side effects was that you do things in a sleep state but you are physically awake. I should have listened to the Holy Spirit because the Holy Spirit was telling me not to take the medication, but the nurse insisted so I took it.

I went to sleep with my wife sleeping in the bed next to me. In the middle of the night I got up and started taking out all of the tubes, and then I decided to take a shower. I have no recollection of these events. My wife indicated that I went for a walk in the shower and she heard the commotion and realized that I had disconnected the tubes. so the nurse said come quickly, there is a problem. In the meantime, I am in the shower taking my time as if it's a beautiful day in the neighborhood. I did not know that I was actually injuring myself and about to pass out. I injured myself. If my wife hadn't been there I don't know what would have happened, but the Holy Spirit said to her you need to be here. I later learned that this medication had a similar effect on others around the world including situations where persons left their homes in the middle of the night driving while fast asleep.

The Holy Spirit brings us wisdom and revelation. He reveals some things to you that nobody else can reveal. 1 Corinthians 2:10 says, these are the things God has revealed to us by his Spirit. Some things you will only get by revelation of the Spirit. The Spirit searches all things. The Spirit knows everything and can figure out anything. The Spirit searches things it says, even the deep things. Sometimes you have to go deep. The shallows are not going to work.

Sometimes you have to get on your knees or walk around praying in tongues. Sometimes when we have our prayer meeting we walk around praying in the Spirit. Why? We want to go deeper. It says, for who knows a person's thoughts except their own Spirit within them. In the same way, no one knows the thoughts of God except the Spirit of God.

If you want to know what God is thinking; if you want to know how to figure out your situation; if you want to know how to get resolution; that is what the Gift of the Holy Spirit is for. It says it searches the deep things of God and sometimes we need some deep things because the shallow things cannot help us. What the Holy Spirit does is He brings about increased discernment. Your discernment level corresponds to your spiritual activity. If you don't pray in the Spirit then you don't get the benefits. That is why the Apostle Paul said, "I pray in tongues more than you all". Why? Because he wanted to have that level of discernment. I want to have that relationship. I want to have that power. I want to have these things happen in my life so I keep praying in the Spirit. He increases your discernment so that you can see things. The Holy

Spirit on the Earth is actually the power of attorney for God.

If you have a relative and they can no longer operate properly in a particular environment, they give you power of attorney so you are able to make decisions on their behalf. The Holy Spirit is the power of attorney of God on the Earth. We have access to God through this power of attorney.

There is a song based upon Psalm 91 that states, My help comes from the Lord. Your help comes from the Holy Spirit. Today we all need help. Our help on the Earth comes through the Holy Spirit. The reason the Gift of the Holy Spirit was given is so that His power can operate in us so that whatever we need we have a power tool that other people don't have. We have someone we can call on that other people, who are not affiliated or connected to God, cannot call. They do not have the access to the Holy Spirit.

For some people when they have a problem the only thing that they have is a bottle or a pipe. They say let me do something or drink something or smoke something to take away the pain. What they do not realize is that the thing they are drinking is listed as wines and spirits. Now that is a spirit indeed but it is not the Holy Spirit. They take that spirit and they put that spirit in them and the result is more problems. This reminds me of the story about a drunken man who said one time he was trying to drown his problems by drinking alcohol. One of his friends confronted him and told him that when you drink alcohol that is not going to drown your problem, instead it is going to teach them how to swim.

The Holy Spirit is there to solve the problem. Correct things. When I need help my help comes from the Lord through the Holy Spirit, through the Baptism of the Holy Spirit and the personal tool of speaking and praying in tongues.

SUMMARY

In summary, remember these important points.

Insight number one: the Holy Spirit was present but not in us.

Insight number two: the role of the Holy Spirit was not released until Pentecost.

So until Pentecost the Holy Spirit was not released onto the Earth as a permanent resident. Some of you may remember the teaching that Dr. Munroe did many years ago. He talked about the Holy Spirit being the governor. In other words the resident authority to make things happen on the Earth.

Insight number three: the Holy Spirit was released, but we have to understand the functions of the Holy Spirit. What are some of these functions?

1. **The Holy Spirit is a Comforter.** Jesus called the Holy Spirit the Comforter. What does the Comforter do? The Comforter comforts you. Whatever you have been through the Holy Spirit is there to comfort you and to give you peace. The Holy Spirit is also referred to as the Spirit of Peace. Sometimes you need peace in your mind. You don't need money. You don't need anything. All you need is some peace. The Holy Spirit is there to deliver the peace.

2. **The Holy Spirit is also a Guide.** Jesus puts it this way, He said He will guide you into all truth. When we think about a guide, the Holy Spirit is like a GPS (Global Positioning System). Recently I was driving from Atlanta to Charlotte and I

had the GPS turned on. I thank God for that GPS because without it I wouldn't have known where I was going. I remember we got to a spot where there was a traffic jam. All we saw for miles and miles and miles were 18 wheelers. Then the GPS started talking to us and said I have found a way. Can you imagine? I mean you know it still boggles my mind what man has been able to do but you see man only duplicates what God has already done. You see the GPS is like man's invention of the Holy Spirit but the only thing is it doesn't really have the power that the Holy Spirit has. It has information but it has limited power. So the GPS says to me I have found a way and I say thank God you found a way because that line looked so long and the GPS told us to turn right. We went so far and my wife said do you think we need to turn here? I said I don't know for sure but just listen to the GPS.

Just wait on the GPS. You have to listen and wait on the Holy Spirit. You have to listen to the right voice because you know if you jumped the gun you could get off track. So here we were, in a very rural area of North or South Carolina and the GPS said go down a few blocks. We went through a town that looked like it might have had seven people, in the whole town. It was so small they didn't even have a stop light, but the GPS knew which way to go. The GPS said follow me.

The Holy Spirit is our GPS. Listen to the voice of the Holy Spirit because if you don't listen to the voice of the Holy Spirit you will be lost. Because we listened to the GPS we didn't get lost. There were a couple times where I felt like I needed to turn but I said no, I just listened to the GPS.

Now can you imagine as we are trying to find our way if the GPS gives wrong directions? You would be in trouble! But, the Holy Spirit is our GPS. The

Holy Spirit will tell you not to take the road that leads you in the wrong direction. Some of you know what I am talking about. The Holy Spirit spoke to you and said don't do that and then you decided to override the GPS. Well you know I have decided that's the worst thing in the world to say to God I have decided because where were you when the worlds were being formed. Who gave you a voice? Jesus said I gave you the Holy Spirit to get direction. Who are you to decide to get directions from another source when Jesus already told you how to get direction?

So this GPS was our guide. We went through all these tiny roads, but then we came back to the highway. The GPS said now go on 85, and I said praise the Lord. We got around the traffic because we listened to the voice of the GPS. The Holy Spirit is our guide. He gives you direction in life. That's why you have to pray and be in touch with the Holy Spirit because you see some of us don't want to be in touch with the Holy Spirit. We want to be guided without paying the price. We want to listen to all kinds of voices.

The other function of the Holy Spirit is power. Sometimes you need power. It is good to have a guide but the GPS that talks to you gives you direction, but it does not give you power. The Holy Spirit will not only give you direction, He will give you the power to get where you need to go. That is why we need the Holy Spirit. **We need all the functions of the Holy Spirit. We need the Helper. We need the Comforter. We need the Guide and we need the power.** The Holy Spirit is the authorizing agent. Jesus said when you pray and you believe when it happens on the Earth the Holy Spirit is the one who authorizes it on Earth because the Holy Spirit is the authorizing agent on Earth. Whatever happens on the Earth the power of the Holy Spirit goes into effect and causes things to happen. That's why the Bible says pray in the Holy Spirit. Why do you pray in the Holy Spirit? Because you want to be charged up with the

Holy Spirit power. You know sometimes people say, "Why are you Speaking in Tongues?" Read the Bible. The Bible said I Speak in Tongues because I am being edified. Edified means to power up. To charge. Sometimes you need a charge.

The Holy Spirit will answer the questions and provide the guidance like Jesus did when He was on Earth. When Jesus said the Holy Spirit will come to help you what He was saying is you know the same answers that I gave you on Earth now without me being present you will get the same answers because the Holy Spirit will be the one who will provide the answers. The Holy Spirit will drop things into your spirit. You know sometimes you are praying and you are meditating and you are wondering what to do and then all of a sudden you receive confirmation.

Ephesians 5:18 puts it like this,

> *"Do not be drunk with wine, but be filled with the Spirit."*

You see, some of us have substituted the Holy Spirit for wines and spirits. We have substituted the Holy Spirit for Hennessy, whiskey or vodka. Wrong spirit. You need to be drunk on the right thing. He says, and do not be drunk with wine, wherein there is dissipation or excess, but be filled with the Spirit. **It's time to be filled with the Spirit. Ask the Holy Spirit to fill your life.**

The Holy Spirit is potent because the Holy Spirit possesses the power of God. The Holy Spirit is God. He is God manifested in the flesh from the spirit realm. It says the Holy Spirit power is potent because He is the power of God residing in us. The Holy Spirit is actually God with us. When Jesus was on Earth his name was Emmanuel, meaning "God with us". He was God with us in one person through the Holy Spirit. God is now in all of us. When Jesus was on the Earth the Holy Spirit had one house. Now the Holy Spirit has as many houses as are available. **"To as many as received Him** to them He gave the power to become the sons of God" John 1.12.

MAKE SURE YOU UTILIZE THE GIFT CORRECTLY

Sometimes people mix up the Holy Spirit, but the Apostle Paul was explaining there's a protocol for the Holy Spirit. There's a way you deal with the Holy Spirit. There's a way you apply the Holy Spirit in your life and once you understand what the Word says about the Holy Spirit you can function effectively.

I remember I went to a church when I had just become a Christian. It must have been only after one week. We went to the church and everybody in the church was **"having the Holy Spirit"**. I was new to the faith but I figured out that this was not the Holy Spirit but they didn't figure it out. I remember there was one fella who went to the pole, a hard wooden pole and he started banging his head on the pole. I mean banging his head! I thought to myself, what in the world is this dude dealing with. He thought He was having the Holy Spirit. Sometimes what people have done is confuse the Holy Spirit with their emotions. What the Apostle Paul was doing is saying here is the protocol.

So not only was the guy banging his head on the wall but another guy ran from the back of the church to the front on top of the pews and then he ran back. Afterward they called me up for prayer. I was saying to myself how do I get out of this? I stood up in front of the guy and he placed his hand on my head and said, "You feel it?" At first I said no, I do not feel it. When he hit me, again I said yeah I feel it, just so I could get away from him. He was asking me if I felt the Holy Ghost. I wasn't sure which ghost it was, maybe Casper the friendly ghost but it was not the Holy Ghost.

PLEASE FOLLOW THESE STEPS

1. Learn about the role and function of the Holy Spirit.

2. Pray and ask God to give you the Baptism of the Holy Spirit with the evidence of Speaking in Tongues (this may be at the altar with a trained prayer counselor or at home on your own).

3. Thank him for giving you the Holy Spirit and rest assured that he has honored your request.

4. Expect to experience the Holy Spirit's power in your life.

5. Exercise the Gift of Speaking in Tongues daily for edification and all the situations you face in life.

6. Learn the protocols for using the gift, both the public and private protocols.

7. Do as the Apostle Paul stated, pray in the Spirit (in Tongues) and with understanding (your natural language).

8. Stay edified (built up and charged through the Holy Spirit).

SCRIPTURES ABOUT THE BAPTISM OF THE HOLY SPIRIT AND SPEAKING IN TONGUES

Acts 2:1-47

When the day of Pentecost arrived, they were all together in one place. And suddenly there came from heaven a sound like a mighty rushing wind, and it filled the entire house where they were sitting. And divided tongues as of fire appeared to them and rested on each one of them. And they were all filled with the Holy Spirit and began to speak in other tongues as the Spirit gave them utterance.

Acts 1:5

For John baptized with water, but you will be baptized with the Holy Spirit not many days from now.

Acts 2:38

Peter said to them, "Repent, and each of you be baptized in the name of Jesus Christ for the forgiveness of your sins; and you will receive the gift of the Holy Spirit."

Matthew 3:11

"As for me, I baptize you with water for repentance, but He who is coming after me is mightier than I, and I am not fit to remove His sandals; He will baptize you with the Holy Spirit and fire."

Acts 1:4

Gathering them together, He commanded them not to leave Jerusalem, but to wait for what the Father had promised, "Which," He said, "you heard of from Me."

Acts 2:4

And they were all filled with the Holy Spirit and began to speak with other tongues, as the Spirit was giving them utterance.

Acts 19:2

He said to them, "Did you receive the Holy Spirit when you believed?" And they said to him, "No, we have not even heard whether there is a Holy Spirit."

Acts 1:8

"But you will receive power when the Holy Spirit has come upon you; and you shall be My witnesses both in Jerusalem, and in all Judea and Samaria, and even to the remotest part of the Earth."

Luke 3:16

John answered and said to them all, "As for me, I baptize you with water; but One is coming who is mightier than I, and I am not fit to untie the thong

of His sandals; He will baptize you with the Holy
Spirit and fire."

Luke 24:49

And behold, I am sending forth the promise of My
Father upon you; but you are to stay in the city until
you are clothed with power from on high."

Acts 19:6

And when Paul had laid his hands upon them, the
Holy Spirit came on them, and they began speaking with tongues and prophesying.

Acts 19:1-6

It happened that while Apollos was at Corinth,
Paul passed through the upper country and came
to Ephesus, and found some disciples. He said to
them, "Did you receive the Holy Spirit when you
believed?" And they said to him, "No, we have not
even heard whether there is a Holy Spirit." And
he said, "Into what then were you baptized?" And
they said, "Into John's baptism."

Acts 2:1-4

When the day of Pentecost had come, they were all together in one place. And suddenly there came from heaven a noise like a violent rushing wind, and it filled the whole house where they were sitting. And there appeared to them tongues as of fire distributing themselves, and they rested on each one of them.

Jude 1:20

But you, beloved, building yourselves up on your most holy faith, praying in the Holy Spirit.

Romans 8:26

In the same way, the Spirit also helps our weakness; for we do not know how to pray as we should, but the Spirit Himself intercedes for us with groanings too deep for words.

Acts 1:4-5

Gathering them together, He commanded them not to leave Jerusalem, but to wait for what the Father had promised, "Which," He said, "you heard of from Me; for John baptized with water, but you will be baptized with the Holy Spirit not many days from now."

Acts 10:44-46

While Peter was still speaking these words, the Holy Spirit fell upon all those who were listening to the message. All the circumcised believers who came with Peter were amazed, because the gift of the Holy Spirit had been poured out on the Gentiles also. For they were hearing them Speaking with Tongues and exalting God.

1 Corinthians 14:2

For one who speaks in a tongue does not speak to men but to God; for no one understands, but in his Spirit he speaks mysteries.

Luke 11:13

If you then, being evil, know how to give good gifts to your children, how much more will your heavenly Father give the Holy Spirit to those who ask Him?"

John 14:16-17

I will ask the Father, and He will give you another Helper, that He may be with you forever; that is the Spirit of truth, whom the world cannot receive, because it does not see Him or know Him, but you know Him because He abides with you and will be in you.

John 7:39

But this He spoke of the Spirit, whom those who believed in Him were to receive; for the Spirit was not yet given, because Jesus was not yet glorified.

Acts 2:38-39

Peter said to them, "Repent, and each of you be baptized in the name of Jesus Christ for the forgiveness of your sins; and you will receive the gift of the Holy Spirit. For the promise is for you and your children and for all who are far off, as many as the Lord our God will call to Himself."

Acts 1:8

But you will receive power when the Holy Spirit has come upon you, and you will be my witnesses in Jerusalem and in all Judea and Samaria, and to the end of the earth.

Matthew 3:11

I baptize you with water for repentance, but he who is coming after me is mightier than I, whose sandals I am not worthy to carry. He will baptize you with the Holy Spirit and fire.

Acts 2:4

And they were all filled with the Holy Spirit and began to speak in other tongues as the Spirit gave them utterance.

Romans 8:26

Likewise the Spirit helps us in our weakness. For we do not know what to pray for as we ought, but the Spirit himself intercedes for us with groanings too deep for words.

John 15:26

"But when the Helper comes, whom I will send to you from the Father, the Spirit of truth, who proceeds from the Father, he will bear witness about me."

John 14:26

But the Helper, the Holy Spirit, whom the Father will send in my name, he will teach you all things and bring to your remembrance all that I have said to you.

Acts 8:14-20

Now when the apostles at Jerusalem heard that Samaria had received the word of God, they sent to them Peter and John, who came down and prayed for them that they might receive the Holy Spirit, for he had not yet fallen on any of them, but they had only been baptized in the name of the Lord Jesus. Then they laid their hands on them and they received the Holy Spirit.

John 14:17

Even the Spirit of truth, whom the world cannot receive, because it neither sees him nor knows him. You know him, for he dwells with you and will be in you.

1 Corinthians 14:2-5

He who speaks in a tongue does not speak to men but to God, for no one understands *him;* however, in the spirit he speaks mysteries. But he who prophesies speaks edification and exhortation and comfort to men. He who speaks in a tongue edifies himself, but he who prophesies edifies the church. I wish you all spoke with tongues, but even more that you prophesied; [a]for he who prophesies *is* greater than he who speaks with tongues, unless indeed he interprets, that the church may receive edification.

1 Corinthians 14:14-15

For if I pray in a tongue, my spirit prays, but my understanding is unfruitful. What is *the conclusion* then? I will pray with the spirit, and I will also pray with the understanding. I will sing with the spirit, and I will also sing with the understanding.

1 Corinthians 14:22-25

Therefore tongues are for a sign, not to those who believe but to unbelievers; but prophesying is not for unbelievers but for those who believe. Therefore if the whole church comes together in one place, and all speak with tongues, and there come in *those who are* uninformed or unbelievers, will they not say that you are [f]out of your mind? But if all prophesy, and an unbeliever or an uninformed person comes in, he is convinced by all, he is convicted by all. And thus the secrets of his heart are revealed; and so, falling down on *his* face, he will worship God and report that God is truly among you.

www.ingramcontent.com/pod-product-compliance
Lightning Source LLC
Chambersburg PA
CBHW070932120626
46546CB00004B/1397